The Millennial Woman

Conquer Your Queendom

BY
TERRI LISELLE KISS

This book is dedicated to my Heavenly Father,

my wonderful, supportive mother,

and to all of the hearts that never gave up.

Table of Contents

Introduction

There are many different ways to achieve success and levels of success; however, success is based on your perspective. This book will first and foremost identify and reshape the barriers that may hinder you from achieving and accomplishing your goals. To change the outside of your life is to reshape the beliefs and the mentality that are keeping you where you are today. What does it take to become the better woman that you want to be tomorrow? It takes changing something today. And this book is it: a ticket, key, a portal to a new way of viewing life and of actually purposefully putting it all into practice. It's our actions that make us who we are, not only by dreaming about them but also by doing them. So dive into this resource, and become the woman that you are meant to be and that our ancestors have dreamt of being for over the last 1000 years.

It's time to shine, as we are the new millennial women of the information age.

I've been in situations and circumstances that have seemed as though there was no way out. I've been unhappy in the past for not attaining dreams that I've set time and time again. I've been stuck at dead-end jobs, lived aimlessly, and no matter what I did, from my entrepreneurial activities to applying to the best schools in the country, nothing seemed to work. My businesses weren't where I wanted them to be, and Ivy League was out of the question for school.

Nothing was going right, until the day when I realized that I must keep calm, be still, and allow a great plan to unfold. I am literally living out my dreams. I got accepted to the legendary fashion design school in the US, Parsons, The New School of Fashion Design, worked as a consultant in a fashion design firm, and later through my real estate and building up my business skills, I gained financial independence. Due to my past efforts, now the fruit is starting to show! My handbag design has been featured in British Vogue, GQ and Tatler Magazine, and it's just the beginning. :) I look forward to sharing some of my thoughts and epiphanies in this book with you.

As we are women in the digital age, I'm sure that the old term, Queen, still has its place in our hearts.

So, what shall Your Majesty learn in order to conquer the great lands? I shall show thee. ;-)

Stay tuned,

Liselle Kiss

Inspirational designer

CHAPTER 1

Conquer Thy Court

_____o_____

> *How to conquer your emotions and live fearlessly.*

ost of our situations result from circumstances that are outside of our control, which can leave us thinking: "Really, why must I go through this?" As a matter of fact, this is the sole reason why we are usually uncomfortable in the current situations that we end up. There are other forces that are more powerful than our external circumstances. I'm talking about our deep thoughts of what goes on in our minds and hearts. It is our thoughts that actually takes us to the places that we find ourselves.

I remember when I wondered why "life happened" sometimes. I didn't understand why I was failing or not being up where I wanted to be. I did the things that society said I should do – finish high school, go to college, get a good job, etc. And in the midst of that, I went through a bad dating relationship that took the life out of me, good and bad. So my emotions were unstable, and I allowed life to dictate how I ought to feel. I felt Life was the ventriloquist, and I was just a cute puppet, just moving along without control. Luckily, a great thing happened. I became so uncomfortable that I decided to find out exactly what it was that made me feel uncomfortable.

Your Majesty's tip: Sometimes it's uncomfortable to call out your enemy because there will surely be a great war.

So, you must be wondering, who is the enemy? Well I'm glad you asked. Let me introduce you to some of the members of your court: Sir Doubt, Sir Fear, and The Duke and Duchess of Discontent and Jealousy.

I've given them titles because, well, they weren't given titles by themselves... they obviously somehow were given the right to stand before you and give you their suggestions of how to rule the queendom of your mind. Certainly, there was a coup d'etat that occurred without your knowledge. "Life happened," that's the mantra of those subjects in your court. So, how must we regain the authority given to us by God to be the ruler of our inner court? We must know the enemy's nature and take them out.

Sir Doubt

At times, our future will look so lovely and bright – until Sir Doubt sweeps us off our feet. I know, he sounds like an ex, but isn't that what doubt does to us? Why can't we just break up with him? Lol.

It's almost the same solution as getting rid of a bad boyfriend – break up and never look back. Yes, this does take strength, although I have a solution that is better than random strength from the air, and that is… Habit.

Habit is a loyal servant and frienemy (friend and potential enemy). It all depends on how you want to treat your friend. Habit can be your loyal best friend or your worst enemy. Let's keep Habit close and treat her kindly. Habit watches your actions and listens to your thoughts in order to make sure that you *do more of what you do* and *think*, in a subconscious manner.

In order to call Habit before you, you must make a conscious effort to create a new thought or action, so that Habit can learn what to do. Therefore, next time that Sir Doubt knocks on your door in the middle of the night or during the day, just decide to not pay attention to him. So, please ignore Sir Doubt's text messages and voicemails, because there's nothing left to say. Simply ignore the

6

doubtful thoughts that cause you to feel inadequate. Aren't there better things to think about anyway? Isn't it interesting that we can only think *one thought at a time*? So, why not choose to change your Thought to something more productive?

Doubting thoughts can creep on us if we are unaware that our minds can drift without knowing it. It's important to catch what you're thinking about when the mind is idle. Usually in these moments, I tend to let my mind focus on something that I want it to think about. I might pull out my tablet to play with an app to practice French, or pull out a good book to come up with new ideas. These little tricks help. Our mind wants to be kept occupied most of the time, so feed it with mind food that you want to produce within yourself.

So where do these doubtful thoughts come from? Well, for starters, *lingering on a bad thought is a bad habit*. True, doubt can be used as a precaution against risk, but I'm talking about the doubt that bears no fruit, the doubt that has nothing to show for, the doubt that tells you that you don't know how to do something, commit, or complete a worthy task. Although doubt is a child of fear, doubt is much more subtle. Even at times, knowing too much of something can lead to doubt, causing a closed mind. You have to know when to *use* Doubt and not let Doubt use you.

Your Majesty's tactic: Know that you don't know, and carry on.

A great way to deflect doubt, is to doubt doubt (not a typo :-D). Just know that you don't know. There are events and circumstances that are unforeseen. Although, by envisioning the outcome of how you want it to end up, you'll get there eventually. So, after doubt has left the building, there are ways to protect the fortress of your mind. You will actually need to use this unforeseen force called Faith to deflect doubt. That is believe in yourself that you are able to doubt the negative thought, that you have the faith that you don't need that doubt. Once faith has replaced doubt, your bestie, Habit, can start laying out the foundation.

It takes about 21 days to create a solid habit, so your persistence is needed. Here are 3 habits that must be laid firmly:

1. Keep your goal in mind,
2. Believe the goal is *already completed,*
3. Take action to prove yourself right.

When I decided to attend fashion school and live in New York, the first thing that I did was let the people that were close to me know that I was going to leave my hometown of beautiful sunny Miami, Florida, to the icy concrete jungle of New York City. As my friends and family were happy for me, they asked me when I was leaving or when I would get accepted to my school. They also wondered where I was going to live or work. I frankly, hadn't thought of those things because I knew that I was going to live in New York and attend my dream school. I coolly let them all know that I hadn't applied yet, wasn't sure when I was leaving, and that I needed their full support and faith with my decision. Deep down inside, I had no doubt that I would make it.

To keep this amount of certainty, I had to give up a few things to gain my prize. *I only told my goals to the few people* that I knew who weren't negative nancies, who were already happy internally themselves, and *were genuinely happy* for any of my past successes. I also made sure that I isolated myself from being fed negativity. I stopped watching the news, started to listen to peaceful, uplifting music, cheered myself on, and thanked God every morning for living in NYC and attending my dream fashion school – all prior to applying to Parsons. I then, in my spare time, built myself a home-based fashion-school curriculum to prepare myself as a student. I then taught myself how to draw fashion figures from watching YouTube videos, studied French, learned about fashion trends and the fashion business, and with the new sewing machine that my mom surprised me with, I taught myself how to sew even though I already knew how to sew by hand. This was a brand new experience.

Since I had no prior education for fashion design, it sounds like a far-fetched dream, right? It sounds so. Even though I sketched outfits since I was a little girl, and even handsewed ripped jeans and upcycled it to a jean jacket at 12, I never would've thought this dream would be real at the age of 23. Though, my passion for designing clothing wouldn't stop me. I saw my future life, and I was certain that there would be nothing to hold me back. Certainty extinguishes doubt 100%.

Sir Fear

Just when you think Sir Doubt has finally given up, he comes back with Sir Fear to remind us of our fears. Why? *It's because fear is paralysis to the mind.* When there is fear, the body is only concerned about how to survive. So, if there is any hint of fear in any course of action we take, of course, we will be unable to move forward, as now the mind is in survival mode. Let's not let fear take a hold of our emotions. We are already emotional at times, so let's learn how to control fear. Sir Fear is a dark knight on a black horse. He looks mighty and terrifying once he is on his high horse. Well, I have a scepter to give you to knock Sir Fear off his high horse. Let's shed some light on what fear is.

In response to the anatomy of fear, HowStuffWorks.com mentions that "Human beings have the sometimes unfortunate gift of anticipation, and we anticipate terrible things that might happen – things we have heard about, read about or seen on TV." It is this "gift of anticipation" that is the foundation that allows us to fear. Therefore, instead of using the "gift of anticipation" for fear, let's use this gift of anticipation to create a new reality.

When it comes to Sir Fear, not acknowledging him, unlike Sir Doubt, isn't the best solution. As easy as it is to disregard single doubting suggestions, Fear has been built on a cluster of doubting suggestions. To tear this bad habit of Sir Fear apart, you must first acknowledge the fear and then know that this presence of fear should have nothing to do with you. Why should a queen be fearful of the future? A queen is hopeful for the future of her queendom.

Your Majesty's highlighted point: A ray of hope diminishes the darkness of fear.

It is the light of hope that diminishes the darkness of fear. So, keep your head up, beautiful one, there is always light when there is darkness. It's just very important to call out that light. It is this hope that allows you to see the light at the end of a dark tunnel. Hope is important to hold on to. So, let's light the fire and torch darkness. Think of the things that were hoped for but were lost in darkness. Write down and rewrite those dreams. I'm sure some of those dreams will find their way back to you.

Now that we know of Sir Fear, there's a couple in your court that are just… ugh! Ok… your Majesty, you must be aware of…..

The Duke And Duchess Of Discontent And Jealousy

Yes, they are the couple that talks behind Your Majesty's back! Of course, they want to dabble in your shining light, so they must sneak in some of their negative thoughts and beliefs to get a grip on your own valuable thoughts. Before we declare, "off with their heads!" – let's find out who they really are….

The Duke Of Discontent

Sometimes discontent will blind you to what is really important *right in front of you*. Sometimes everything seems to go so perfect; however, there is this little nudge in your gut that keeps you discontented and unthankful. I know there are some days where everything is going the way that it should be, but I still can get these thoughts of being unhappy. It is such a perplexing situation! Maybe everything is going well; however, there is just that one thing that is missing, whether that be love, money, or recognition, or what that other person has on the internet.

Discontent is everywhere among us. Most use it as a conversation starter, i.e., "It's so hot outside/inside." Others use it as a way of life, i.e., "Well, you can't get everything, can you?" Even though the two examples are subtle and frequently used, this subtle use is the invisible toxic gas to our mindset. Why is discontent so accepted?

I remember one of my mentors used to ask me the question, "How was your day today, Terri?"

I would respond, "Good, all right."

Then he would reply, "What was it, Today, that you were thankful for?"

13

Already in a crummy mood from his persistency, I would respond, "Ah, well I woke up and went to work."

Then he would respond, "And?"

"Uh.. We did well at work, working on closing a deal."

"And?"

"I had a good lunch."

"And...?"

As my mentor would jolt my mind to think of things that made me feel thankful, I couldn't feel as if I had just a normal day. I felt empowered, like this day was one of the greatest in my life. I even felt more excited for what would happen in the future. I then realized that the feeling of thankfulness deters all feelings of discontent. Thankfulness is another light in the darkness of Discontent. Imagine if you were only to live a life of discontent. How on earth would you be able to see any sort of opportunities that presented themselves?

If you were to stay in a state of discontent, then no matter what the circumstances were, whether good or bad, you would remain in the same state of discontent. You would be unable to take advantage of anything else, because there is nothing else. Opportunities cannot be seen with Sir

Discontent. So do not take his advice! Just thank him for the thought and move on.

A way to jump out of the feeling of discontent is not only to be in a state of thankfulness but also to be in a state of giving. Giving your time to help others is another great way of forgetting about your bad circumstances and help those less fortunate. So, a great exercise would be to volunteer frequently to a cause that is worthwhile. This could be joining a breast cancer walk or helping out an old friend to clean her garage, etc. – anything to lend a helping hand. Even giving some advice online without expecting anything back is a good way to be thankful.

The Duchess Of Jealousy

Ooh Jealousy, I'm sure we've all felt the heart-gripping reach of jealousy. Some forms are extreme; others are slight... Though, one thing they have in common is that Jealousy can become an obsession. The Duchess of Jealousy is obsessed with herself and your court! You see, Jealousy is an extreme form of discontent. As Fear is a cluster of doubt, Jealousy is a cluster of discontent. This is of course, a general statement, not about a drama over, well you know, men. I'm keying in on how jealousy can affect through your way of living. Seeing a top performer in an organization or sports team, a celebrity

15

or influencer can lead us in a state of jealousy, if we are not aware. Even a best friend getting the latest new outfit or car can stir up some feelings. The jealousy stems from, the unanswered question of "Why Not Me?"

Here's what the Duchess of Jealousy tells Your Majesty often: "Why doesn't Your Majesty see the beauty of the other queendoms? I'm sure you'll have splendor like the others, one day. Maybe."

So subtle, and it looks harmless, but oooh, isn't she so conniving? Let's not get too heated... I've got a remedy to shut her down.

One of the books I read, and highly recommend, *Thought Vibration* by William Walker Atkinson, suggested, in the context of removing jealousy, to "Think of your higher nature and laugh." I thought that that was rather peculiar. It reminded me that I didn't need to compare myself to anybody. Comparing yourself to others is exactly what the Duchess of Jealousy wants you to do! She knows jealousy starts from there!

I recall years ago, when I was striving to be promoted to a new payment level in a network marketing company, there were others that weren't even in the business for as long as I was who surpassed me by leaps and bounds. I felt inadequate at times because, with my business degree background and the number of hours I'd put in the business, I surely felt that I deserved more, especially in that certain time span. I didn't realize that, through me comparing myself to others, I was holding myself back from looking forward and keeping my eyes on the prize. The Duchess of Jealousy was really starting to get to me.

Certainly, I still pushed and at times held back because I didn't want to be in the business for the wrong reasons. Money and recognition at times can consume us, more than what we think we should allow. I had to build my self-worth gradually over time, so that I wouldn't be consumed with others' approval. So eventually, through trial and error, I realized that the networking marketing business I was in was not for me. Although I made valuable connections, who helped me to accomplish my dreams in that near future, I left because I realized that working that business was not aligned with my long-term goals. Network marketing relies heavily on the actions of other people, and I just wasn't the person to build a business based on recruiting people. I didn't want to race anymore with others to do this, I wanted to find my own lane and compete with myself.

Your Majesty's tip: Life can seem like a race. It is better to look forward at the finish line, rather than looking to the side to see the brand name of your competitor's sportsgear. That would just cause an accident on the track, and trust me, that race of yours will be delayed or unfinished.

So, think highly of yourself. There is abundance out there beyond the queendom of your mind. Think bigger. There are better and more abundant ideas, relationships, people, and opportunities. When did the word "opportunity" get scarce? See, the word still exists, and that means opportunity will always exist. Yep! (My rational to boost you up!)

The Mirror On The Wall & The Self-Image

One thing I realized that is very important is the perception that you give to your Self-image. Yes, your physical image is important to you, right? You must make sure you look normal enough, with each of your own sets of beauty standards, to show that you care enough about the way we look. However, even though you may spend plenty of time fixing up your outer beauty, you have probably over time, neglected to tell yourself who you really are. This is your Self-Image. As an inspirational fashion designer for my label Liselle Kiss, I try to design not only for the wearer, but to maintain a positive Self-image for the wearer through my design bundles like this book you're reading or my online inspirational courses. The fashion industry is a beautiful industry yet can promote vanity all too much. You can style yourself on the outside, while you style your Self-image and recreate yourself deliberately with purpose. Your Self-image is affected by the way you view yourself, so you must style your Self-image daily too!

When I wake up in the morning to get dressed and carefully apply my makeup, I'm also carefully examining the way that I'm feeling in the morning. I ask myself, "How am I feeling? happy? frustrated? content? overwhelmed?" Then, as I'm examining my thoughts and emotions in the morning, I tell myself how I want my day to be. I look at myself in the mirror, smile, and tell myself to get excited for the blessed day ahead! Then, my day is already off to a great start. At times, I'll even talk to myself of what I want to hear, like: "Good job, girly! You're on your way!" or even, "I can't wait to see what exciting and amazing things will happen today!" Just by voicing positive sayings creates a new energy around you that will be the armor that you need for your day.

So, the tone and movement of my day is already set. I've already styled my Self-image that I want to portray. Therefore, if there is an unfortunate incident in my day that allows me to feel upset or doubtful, I must be mindful of my emotions and feelings. If it is the feeling of doubt, I then toss the thought away and think of things throughout the day that I'm glad to be working towards. I replace Sir Doubt and think, "progress," and I reward myself according to any level of progress that I achieve that day.

I once decided to work for a telemarketing company, just to improve my sales methodology. I've always been fascinated with sales because it is a profession that feels like a sport. There is mental conditioning to push the limits, as well as making that impactful shot to close the deal. I love to take on challenges to grow my character, and I felt that selling tickets over the phone to people who were not expecting my call was the perfect challenge. :D

So, as I started to make about 30 calls per hour in my lovable cubicle, I would get many people that would hang the phone up on me, get upset, or were just unwilling to hear my pitch. This was detrimental to my Self-image, as I could easily feel unwanted, misunderstood, and futile as an individual, or even as a salesperson in general. I then realized that I was treating my Self-image the wrong way. I was being too hard on myself. So, I then decided to start patting myself on the back after a tough phone call. I mean, I wasn't expecting a manager or my cubicle neighbor to do it for me, so I felt that I should do something silly like pat myself on the back to feel better. Well, that was the catalyst that created my new Self-image. All of a sudden I started to call up the prospects with such enthusiasm about how they deserved to go the concert that I was offering. Eventually, I started to sell 5–6 ticket packages a day, when my peers would sell 1 or 2 in a week. Later on, I showed a few of my peers the mindset needed to control their self-image to close the deals too, and soon their sales also started to increase.

We decided to look at ourselves in the mirror and ask, "Mirror, mirror on the wall, who is the fairest of them all?" Keep in mind that you should first think of being fair to you first by letting go of the blame card. Be easy on yourself, then become fair to them all. And that, my dear is how to become the ruler of the court, the queendom of your mind.

In what ways do you keep yourself cheerful and thankful?

The Millennial Woman Knows About Programming Her Court

The millennial woman is the woman who is a programmer of change and looks forward to updating herself according to her new environment or rather, domain. By building the fortitude of her mind, she can control her feelings and emotions according to her ability to adapt, thereby setting the tone of her new environment. She knows that the future is her present, her present has already past, and her past is fleeting and not worth lingering on, like yesterday's liked photo. When Doubt, Fear, Discontent, or Jealousy shows up on her screen as a pop-up window, she simply deletes it.

CHAPTER 2

Scout Thy Territory

Now that we have the mindset needed to rule our court, we are able to look outside our court and move onto the other lands we can conquer. First, we must send a messenger to scout the territory and then move onto other lands. It is quite important to understand the difference between knowing what is in the queendom and what is outside of the queendom. If we happened to step outside of our territory without knowing what the boundaries are, surely, we will be lost or in danger. Knowing the difference between what you have and what you don't have is important.

Now, let's go and scout the territory your Majesty!

The Conquistador

In 1492, Christopher Columbus left Spain to discover the new land across the Atlantic, and later the Conquistadors followed him to conquer the terrain. It was this Golden Age of Spain that allowed Spain to be ready for the next and new beginning. There were new opportunities, as they found resources in gold, jewels, and other treasures. Soon after, the other European countries followed, and the rest is history.

In order to understand our territory, think of the qualities that Christopher Columbus needed to go forth to the Queen of Spain to get permission to go across the Atlantic. *First, he must have had a sense of curiosity and purposeful determination.* To spark the purpose for success, we must first be open to curiosity. Luckily, in this age of information and being able to Google anything that comes to our mind, curiosity is a helpful friend. Curiosity becomes useful, once a purpose to the curiosity is established.

Knowing The Inside Of The Queendom

You have skills, qualities, talents, and abilities that are unique and special. To identify which of these skills or qualities will prove useful is determined by the amount of time, effort, or giftedness that is placed on each skill. Then it is important to find out *which activity is worth doing*, which makes you so happy that if you weren't paid for it and money were not an issue, you'd be able to continue doing that skill or activity throughout your life.

I remember the first time that I discovered this point of doing more than paid for. It took me a while before I was able to find out what it was that made me special or unique. Right before this time, I worked a full-time sales executive job, around 50 hours a week, in addition to the hours I put in for my network marketing side business. I had a great idea of using one of my skill sets and favorite pastimes of networking to focus on developing business accounts for my side business. After a couple of networking events, I met a gentleman who became one of my close mentors. He asked me what it was that I was working towards. Apparently, at that time, I told him that I wanted to go part-time from my full-time 50-hour week. He asked me if I was doing anything at the moment to get there. I told him that I worked 50 hours a week now, and I was running a side business, so that my side business could replace 50% of my income. As we were both fans of the book, *Law of Success in 16 lessons* by Napoleon Hill, he mentioned the law of doing more than paid for. We spoke further about what defines a "labor of love." A labor of love is defined as a project, job, or task that flows according to your abilities and skill set, while loving that very activity. I told him that at the moment, I was not doing any sort of labor of love, because my side network marketing business was only for making money and was not my labor of love.

A couple of weeks later, I left my full-time status and went part-time to discover this "labor of love." I thought, at the time, that having the extra hours of free time in the week was a great motivation to make more money in the side business that I worked hard on, although, after a while, I realized that there are only so many hours in a day, and even if I worked all day on my side business, I was nowhere near finding my actual labor of love.

So, I then scouted my territory. I enjoyed my part-time life. I brunched on Ocean Drive in South Beach on Monday, attended meetings throughout the week, and enjoyed my new workweek by finding time to relax. Meanwhile, I completely devoted myself to self-development by reading books by Robert Kiyosaki and Napoleon Hill and listened to motivational audios. Everyday, I thought and wrote down what it was that I was interested in accomplishing. I always carried a notebook on me, just in case I suddenly became inspired by a new idea or thought. I sometimes sat out on my back porch to remember what I wanted and replay the thoughts and dreams in my mind that I had always wanted to accomplish.

Think: What is your labor of love, and how would discovering that shape your life?

Discovering The Outside Of The Queendom

After a couple of weeks of searching and working, I eventually started to remember my love for fashion. Yes, I always loved fashion; however, becoming a fashion designer was the dream that I had put off for a couple of years. After college, I worked in the corporate world for numerous years and also ran my own t-shirt and purse business. I never was educated in fashion design, but I knew that I had a knack for it. With this newfound discovery, I realized that although I *possessed the potential skill* for fashion, I had *never really explored the opportunity to work* in fashion. I had to find out what I didn't know about fashion. When asked if I knew the latest designers or if I knew the biographies or strategies of successful designers, I flat-out realized that I knew nothing. The word, "fashion" seemed like that was all I needed to know. So, I went and discovered what I wanted to conquer.

It takes careful thought and reflections to know exactly what it is that you may want to achieve or conquer in your life. Life at times gives us samples of what we may or may not like, just for us to taste and see whether the lifestyle that we choose is for us or not. To find meaning and purpose, we must first give ourselves the opportunity to be open to try out and test these samples. Since we have already blocked out doubt, fear of loss, or any other types of barriers, we are able to chart new waters and explore new opportunities.

Think. What is it that you want? If money wasn't an issue and you knew you couldn't fail, what would you do? What is it that you want to conquer in your life? Write this down now. I could stress more and more about the importance of owning a thinking pad (my name for a notebook) on you most of the time. Our best moments, ideas, inspirations, and thoughts happen when we are idle. It is great to organize our thoughts, find out what we want, like, and plan on having. To dream it, is to live it.

Anticipate The Territory

I have a question, Your Majesty... as Queen, and soon to be Empress, how would the territory look like when you conquer it?

Your Majesty's proverb: "Where there is no vision the people perish." Proverbs 29:18

Visualization is key. There are several techniques I would suggest that work on defining the dream or lifestyle that you want. One of the most powerful techniques that I have seen and used is to create a dream board. That's right. On you next visit at your favorite home goods store, pick up a large poster board with a nice frame, and some magazines. Make sure that these magazines have images or words that make you smile. I love to pick up lifestyle magazines, such as ones about building a dream home, fashion magazines, or success-oriented magazines. Afterwards, I cut out the words and pictures that I would love to have and paste them on my framed poster board. When I completed my dream board, I placed it where I could see it instantly when I woke up and right before I fell asleep. I cut out images of cars, clothes, fashion terms, etc. Over time, I even changed and updated my dream board because I was constantly changing over time and becoming a new person.

Another great way of finding and motivating your purpose is to journal. I love journaling. Note, this is separate from my thinking pad. In my journal, I write experiences to motivate me. In my past, I used to journal about anything that happened throughout my day. Years ago, when I was in a bad dating relationship that took the life out of me, I wrote in my journal sad moments and memories. The entire journal encompassed these moments, and I even mixed in my happy thoughts too. I held onto that journal for about 4 years, *only because I had it for 4 years,* until later I realized that, as I reread my journal entries, I would go back into my unhappy state. *So, I had to throw it away.* I threw it away and later bought a new journal. In this new journal, I promised myself that I would only write good things, and if there was a bad moment, I would write a moment of motivation instead of desolation.

As a millennial woman, in your journal entries, it is important to write some entries that are placed in the future. For example, I wrote entries about my life living in New York City, attending Parsons fashion design school, and meeting new people before I even applied to the school. I was already thanking God for the experience and opportunity of attending such a great school. I wrote in a state of gratitude. I dated my entries the same day as I wrote them, and I defined my self-image. I would write, "I am sooooo excited to attend my dream school and work in fashion in NYC! It is sooo crazy how I am here doing this! The people here are awesome. I love the city, and man, I can't believe it, this is amazing. I am soooo thankful!" It is so very interesting to see that when I look back at these old entries, the majority of them have already come true. Sometimes I'll review the entries and think, "Oh right, I must've written that recently," and when I check, I actually wrote that entry a couple of months before.

Your Majesty's Note on Getting Exactly What You Want:

I know that this can sound new age and like "The Secret" but there is a method to this. The point of this all is having the "faith" that you can have this. This is all part of using your free will and determinism. I have dived in head first before into "The Secret" of believing but that is not enough. You must feel it, like a clench in your chest. Like a warm fire in your heart. You must know it and not see anything else. You have to be excited and happy that it has already happened. Pray in thanksgiving it has already happened. And the most important part for me, is that you have to pray that it's the right thing that you want. We can manifest anything we want, but I usually like to pray to God to ensure that what I want is the right thing. That He will also bless me in the endeavor that I have in my heart. Using your power to do something is good, but taking off the weight of the world and running with God's blessing on top of what you want is a complete other thing. I explain this more in detail with my digital spiritual course Thy Queendom Come: Unlocking God's Purpose Behind the Desires of Your Heart on https://thy-queendom-come.thinkific.com/courses/queendom

If you visualize, write, and speak the things that you want, as long there is a deep and burning desire for your purpose, eventually you will receive them. On those days that

Sir Doubt wants to try to come back and sweep me off my feet, but I look up at the skyscrapers of New York City. I see and visualize the opportunities that God has set before me. It's important to keep on visualizing and dreaming even after accomplishing one goal or dream. Feeling that you already *made* it is the first step to losing it. Stay humble, and realize that it is important to feel that you're *making* it, no matter what state of defeat or success you find yourself in.

A slight tip for Your Majesty: Stay humble and stay thankful whilst conquering the other lands.

How many times do you visualize a day? Set a goal.

Plant Your Flag

After you've seen the terrain and surveyed your land, it is important to plant your flag. In other words, it is important to claim what you want and stick with it. There will be obstacles that may want to take your flag, but you mustn't let go. Keep a sound mind and do not waver. It is quite important to have laser vision to complete the goal. If the mind has more than one thing to focus on, it may not be able to complete the task as efficiently as focusing on one thing at a time. Once there is vision in place for your purpose, it is important to keep looking at the target. Quite a few times with goal setting, I've been so enthusiastic with an idea or vision, that I almost immediately got another idea or vision that was just as fantastic. This *double vision could cause confusion,* until I decided to pick one and then placed the other opportunities on hold.

I remember, when I was younger, I wanted to do all sorts of things all at the same time. I performed with hip-hop dance teams in both high school and college. I dreamt of being a choreographer or being a professional dancer, dancing around the world. In addition to this, I had a desire to be a fashion designer and run a successful business in general. I had to pick my priorities. Even though joining a dancing company or going straight to technical design school after high school graduation were options, I decided to wait and go to college to acquire my bachelor's degree in entrepreneurship. I found out that eventually, the pieces of my dreams started to fall into place. In college, I started my first t-shirt and tote bag business as a corporate promotional product. After graduation, I secured a great full-time job, while continuing my business. Eventually, I became so wrapped up with working at my day job, that I dropped my business. I had to reflect on what my goals and dreams were again after a few years later, because I felt that I had lost my long-term vision. After a few years after graduating college, I remembered my dream of being a fashion designer and moving to NYC. I decided to join a network marketing business for this reason and to learn new marketing practices that I hadn't used before. I also learned how to dream, build, and set goals for myself and for others.

It takes time to realize the path and stick with it. *It is a far greater journey to start building the colony after claiming the territory.* Writing down these goals, seeing the dream board, and visualizing everyday is important to keep your flag planted.

The Neighboring Countries

As a millennial woman, you are living in a time of new possibilities. You will become easily distracted because of these opportunities. Yes, when you look to scout the territory to claim what is yours, there are chances that there are other queendoms out there that want what you want. This doesn't necessarily mean that there is a lack of resources to get what you want, but there will be challenges. There are times and places for things to happen in our lives. Sometimes it may look as if things are not going your way to accomplish a worthwhile dream, but it takes determination and visualization to get what you want. Visualization must be met with action at the appropriate time. Timing is everything.

As the new set of women living at the turn of the century, you are affected by the speed of this new information driven society. I remember a couple of years ago, my mother was a top district sales manager for a major insurance company. She truly enjoyed her job and excelled in every aspect. After the recession hit in 2008, there were major shifts and moves within her company. Her company was bought out, and the new management started to take a significant portion of money from her paycheck to pay for their own recruiting at her expenses. They were obviously looking for ways to fire her and replace her with someone with a lower salary. On top of that, they didn't respect her status of being a woman district manager, as her boss mentioned that she was slacking because she was recently married. So, in effect she had to remember and visualize what she wanted in life. She always mentioned how she wanted to own a business to help the elderly. A couple of months after the new takeover, she left her position in the company to start an elderly caregiving company with her new husband.

No matter what position or place you are in, you may have circumstances that may seem to hinder your opportunities. However these circumstances are usually a wake-up call to your true calling in life. It's important to be a little uncomfortable to be ready for positive change. Change is good as long as you focus this energy into something productive. This is the age of opportunity, an age for taking chances and catapulting from the abyss that some people call stagnation. You control your destiny; you create your future; you will create and continue to discover who you are. Only you will tell yourself who you really are.

The Millennial Woman's Attitude Of Never Settle

New circumstances sometimes happen to shake you up so that you may not be able to settle in a bad situation. Settling for what you don't want and taking what is given to you is as atrocious as letting a neighboring colony take your land and tell you that you can rent it from them. Never settle in all that you do. That even goes down to the candy that you eat. When you ask for Twizzlers at the movie theatres, and you're then given Red Vines, don't take them. Lol. It is as simple as that. :D

Settling is a Habit that can be replaced with Never Settle. Now, lets not get confused with not compromising or negotiating. At times, given the situation, these methods can benefit you. However, feeling like you've given away an important piece of you that will not benefit you at all is frankly settling. Just because you are too comfortable to change the situation, is settling. Settling is a defensive stance, a white flag, and an attitude that the new woman must never have. Why? It's because she creates her own future. She conquers her court and any territory that she sets out to conquer. Once a ruler settles and lacks keen decision-making, that ruler will eventually be handed over. Let's not let our minds be ruled over by the desires and dreams of others. When we are faced with a situation or circumstance that is beyond our control, it is important to be at peace and act coolly before we take action. We will council those who have been in our shoes and those who we admire to get out from a bad settling situation.

Even if we have settled in the past, settling doesn't need to be present in your future. If there is an opportunity that seems unworthy, take it, try it, and make it yours. One day, what you want in life may want you. Test out the horizon, and act like the woman that you want to become. Dress like her. Think like her. Talk like her. And later on, you'll become her. Start the career, business, and family goals you want. Live out the dream. Cheer yourself on. Pat yourself on the back. And conquer thy territory!

CHAPTER 3

Show Mercy In Thy Queendom

The right attitude to network for success.

I t is important to be likable, however, only to the point that you are not being affected in a negative manner like being too passive. So far, I've discussed the internal queendom of your mind, and now, rather, I will key in on the topic of being able to use your ability to socialize in order to create and establish your network for success.

One thing about being a beloved ruler is to show love for others. Sometimes, people get so caught up with their position that they tend to forget those that helped place them there, or they forget that they were in the previous positions in the past. Yes, you want to be successful and gain recognition and merit for what you love to do; however, you must show it off in a manner that is quite pleasing. Yes, although you've been conditioned to flaunt the stuff of this world, it is imperative that you continue to appreciate the

38

little things. It is important to keep humble throughout the process of attaining your dreams. *There are many different reasons and ways why some opportunities come towards others and why others don't, and sometimes it's typically by who you know, not necessarily by what you know.* I'm sure that you've heard this many times. However, it is important to recognize this, not as a disadvantage, but as an advantage to the future opportunities that lie ahead of you.

The Queen Bee

Recently, I was interested in researching what exactly the term "queen bee" came from and how it is related to nature. Although "queen bee" sounds like a cute nickname for a woman that is on top of her game, the real nature of the queen bee in nature is quite surprising. In a beehive, there is only one queen amongst the drones (male bees). Eventually, the queen bee will die, and when that happens, a female bee will be appointed queen... after she kills off all of the other female bees. Whichever female bee is left standing is now the new Queen Bee.

To avoid having our lives being another episode of Gossip Girl, stepping on others, and having them eventually step on us back – let's skip the drama and let's be a Humble Bee. Lol. Although I speak of being a queen throughout this book, I by no means am suggesting being a queen bee. As a matter of fact, it is important to be aware of refraining from the queen bee mindset, because purposely putting someone down to get what you need in life is as close to shooting yourself in the foot as you can get, especially as you attempt to progress in your endeavors in the future. What you do you attract back to you the same way. The way you act is like the honey that attracts the same type of bees. It's better to be a humble bee than a queen bee. You don't want to fight and compete all day. Remember to compete with yourself only.

Your Highness's Grace

"Be Nice" is such a simple term, that I'm sure that we remember hearing it over and over in grade school. ;)

I remember that one of the coolest deans I'd ever met (the Dean of Fashion at Parsons, of course) in my fashion school orientation mentioned 5 points to be successful in the fashion industry. One of his most interesting and intriguing points was his point of "BE NICE." He went on to describe that even though the industry does put individuals in stressful situations, at the end of the day, if he had to hire two people with the same credentials and abilities, he would hire the one that was flat out nice.

Being nice matters. However, what is more important than being just nice, is to develop that as a character trait, not just a mood. I'm quite sure we've experienced situations where some of the people that we encountered were just not consistently nice people. They put on a front of being nice, and then being cold, then being nice again. Perhaps, that person hadn't experienced nice people, or perhaps thought that they needed to show that they were a step ahead of the pack (the queen bee) to exude dominance. Unfortunately, that individual ends up being sort of disliked or untrustworthy, because that person's influence was rooted in intimidation, not necessarily through being genuinely liked. Being liked and having that pleasing personality is more powerful than instilling fear and intimidation into others. Most people want to work with people who they like, not people who they fear. Lol. It just makes life easier that way for others in the long run. So, sometimes situations and circumstances can call for us to not be as nice as we hope to be. It's alright to be assertive if it works for you, or not. However, it is important to keep in consideration other people's feelings. If there is nothing really good to say that is productive, it is better to cool off and then respond accordingly after you've already thought things through.

Pulling out Your Queen of Hearts

It's easier to let go of something once you are out of your shoes. Sometimes, if you are able to see yourself in the shoes or circumstances of others, you are able to show a bit more empathy. And a little bit of empathy goes go a long way. Yes, we all have our problems and circumstances we are involved with. However, life is more than just dealing with our problems. Life is meant to be lived, and problems are sometimes a part of it, not the entire situation.

There was a time when I had a tenant that stopped paying rent for the condo that I owned. As this was the first time that I'd experienced a tenant not paying rent, I gave her 30 days to pay the rent that was owed. This actually caused a delay in my own personal finances, so my personal situation wasn't looking so good. Eventually, after 30 days, I started a lawful process of eviction, and she was quite stubborn and didn't want to leave, even when I placed the first notice on her door. Even though it took her 15 days after to leave, she made sure that she damaged some of my appliances and vandalized my home. This experience was heartbreaking for me. I didn't understand why a person would do such a thing when I gave her ample time to move out. There was a moment that I was just filled with anger against her. I saw that, even though we had an agreement and she said she would leave she still stayed.

I had to come to terms with the moment, and first realize who she was and what I was doing. I realized that sometimes, people have illogical ways and motives that are just beyond our own beliefs and methods. However, *just because someone may seem to act illogically, that doesn't mean that we have to become apathetic to their situation.* Of course, my tenant felt that she would have nowhere to go, and decided to take advantage of the opportunity, no matter what it cost me. And that was something that I had to understand. So even to this day, although I haven't received one cent from her, I understand that it must've been hard for her.

Empathy does bring peace of heart and mind.

Using your Scepter of Forgiveness

Yes, Forgiveness comes right after empathy. It's tough to forgive someone if you're unable to show empathy for that person. Perfection is a quality that is hard to achieve, and of course, many of us have fallen short of perfection. So because you are not all perfect, eventually you can mistakenly hurt someone, or someone can mistakenly or purposefully hurt you. Life is a freeway, and there are accidents, bumper-to-bumper traffic, and hit and runs. Sometimes, the best insurance policy on your heart is to forgive others for what they've done. This is a great way to cleanse the conscience.

Once you have a clear conscience, you are now able to focus on the greater things in life, for you to succeed and be happy, rather than looking back and feeling regret or anger.

Yes, we could have a bad boyfriend or a close loved one that has deeply hurt us or told us that we are unable to succeed to achieve our dreams. As a response, we can go ahead and try to prove them wrong with the evidence of success in our lives. But is that really as conducive for our hearts or for our peace of mind?

It's important to let go, forgive, and let yourself live.

Your Majesty's mantra: Let go, forgive, and let live.

Lift Someone's Spirit

After you've acquired the strength to forgive someone (and yourself), now you have the ability to use your newly acquired royal scepter to lift up someone else's head. Yes, even when you are in a good mood with a good life, and not care about the rest of the world when everything is going quite well, do not let yourself forget about the ones that are down and left behind. Sometimes that extra gesture or smile can completely change someone's life or perspective. That random smile, laughter, or attention to someone can make a person feel significant. You never know what a small thing can do for a person's day.

Usually, when you lift up those around you to feel better and more appreciated, eventually the act of doing that will be reciprocated, especially on those days when you could be feeling better yourself. Everything that goes out has to come back, and that includes the way that you treat others. Living a pleasant life includes being around pleasant people. So, treat others as if they are *all* pleasant. ;-)

Your Majesty's Smiling Grace

Smiling is a happy habit. Not only is smiling a reaction to a positive notion in our environment. It can be used also as a way of creating our environment. Sometimes, throughout your day, you can be so carelessly consumed with stress and matters of your life that there is nothing that can actually make you smile. We can literally sit at our desks, and nothing can make us smile. But there is one thing that can make you smile, even when there is nothing out there that can. And that is you.

Yes you, your Highness. Sometimes forcing a smile can make you actually smile and feel better. I once listened to an audio by Tony Robbins, and he spoke about how our physical body movements can determine our mood and conscious state. He went on to explain that if we have negative body movements, such as slouching or frowning, that is going to show the emotion that we are actually feeling. By knowing this, if we allow ourselves to change our body language into the feelings that we actually want to feel, then we will actually be in a better mood.

So, I decided to adopt this habit of smiling into my daily life and habits. And it works every time. If I want to smile, I smile, and then I feel better about it. Try it. Now is even better… :) smile!

Look at yourself in the mirror and smile from ear to ear. Yes, you will genuinely smile because you feel as if you're silly smiling at yourself, but it doesn't matter anyway, because it worked, and now you are smiling. :D

Your Majesty's proverb: A good smile in a day sets a course in the wind for a better day.

Happiness is Contagious

Who wouldn't want to catch happiness by accident? Lol. Happiness is an attitude that can be chosen and not landed on by accident. Choose to be happy, and do the things that make you overjoyed with love. Even when times get rough and there are things in your way that want to rob you of peace and happiness, *it is important to choose the state of mind of working on feeling better* to be thankful and appreciative. Appreciation is a major catalyst for the level of happiness that you can possibly achieve. It is alright to be content with what you have, *but it is even better to be overjoyed with appreciation with what you have* and not worry about tomorrow. Tomorrow doesn't exist, but today does.

APPOINTING YOUR INNER COURT (Your Royal Posse)

Now that you have accomplished the traits necessary to attract the right people into your life, as well as having already banished out the traitors and negative dukes and duchesses from your court, it is time to appoint those that are in your inner circle. Lol, ahem yes, your Round Table. *These are not only your friends, but they play a significant role in the level of success that you will take part in the future.* < Re-read that last sentence again ;) No, but seriously, "you are what you eat" is as parallel to the statement "you are who your friends are."

So, take a look around... who are your friends or influencers? Are they positive or negative? Genuinely nice or passive aggressive? Do they talk about their dreams and goals, or do they only complain about their jobs? What is their income? What do they read? Who do they listen to? As you're reading these questions, answer these questions for yourself. Who are you, and what do you do? Now think, *who* around you is someone that you want to be? Do you have someone or a group of people with a certain amount of success that you want to achieve? If not, then where do you start to find these kinds of people with ambitions and goals too? Being selective of the company you keep helps you to manage and keep a good Self-image. Your royal posse's habits and abilities can rub off on you just by association.

Your Majesty's Habit: Be Selective and Decisive.

When I left Miami and moved to New York, I had to start from scratch to find a new social life. That was a bit difficult at first because I was so used to calling up friends to meet them in South Beach whenever the mood hit me. However, when I left and moved to a brand new, bigger city, perhaps one of the most notorious cities in the world, I had to be quite cautious while making friends from scratch. Although I was thrilled to start school again and make new friends, I still needed to be selective of the company I kept. The social butterfly in me was being tormented for a while, as I settled in for the move. It takes patience and selection to find the right types of personalities that can make me a better person. So, eventually after a couple of months, I finally met nice, humble, and ambitious people who I felt had the traits and characteristics that I wanted to adopt in myself.

How did you select your Round Table?

Network With the Other Queendoms

A great method of finding people that you would like to become friends with is by finding people that share your interests and that are "doing something." A great tool is www.*Meetup.com*. There you can find interesting groups from kayaking to business investor meetups. Mixing up these groups is a great way to meet all different types of people that can allow you to become very well rounded. I've attended a French Conversation Meetup, just to attempt to practice my French. ;) Now My French is intermediate after leaving the event with a headache attempting to speak the language. Networking with others is an opportunity to learn and harness the skills of others, whilst being in an environment that is meant to push you into being a better human being. Eventually, as you continue to network and meet certain people constantly, they will get to know who you are, and friendships and business partnerships will start to develop.

The first time I was ever introduced to networking was through the Collegiate Entrepreneurship Organization that I participated in in college. One day, a gentleman named Scott Bender, a Networking Guru of the area, spoke at our chapter meeting about the significance of business networking. From that day on, I decided to help him with his networking meetups and networked with the business owners of the Greater Orlando Area. Only 19 at the time, I felt like the youngest person there and was perceived as "cute" rather than a serious attendee. Luckily, from working behind the scenes organizing Scott's networking meetups, I realized that the same people constantly attended. I originally didn't see the significance of who these people attending all the time were, and frankly, I thought that they attended because they were just desperate for business. However, over time, as I started to develop friendships with the members (for the first time having friendships way older than me), I realized that these people were quite successful at what they did. As a matter of fact, these people were quite successful because they networked so much. I had no idea that the friends I was making were Vice President of Promotion or top players in their industry. How naive I was! I was sitting with the people that were going to mentor me into being a better entrepreneur and individual. They were actually quite helpful and genuinely concerned with helping each other succeed. If there was a referral to give or a helping hand to lend, they were there to help each other.

I'm sure time and time again, we've heard the saying "there is no such thing as a self-made millionaire," and frankly, that is true. It takes a team of people that is in your network to succeed. Not all of them are your employees and professionals; some of them are in your inner court.

So, think. Who is cheering you on? Who in your inner court is excited for the things that are happening in your life? Who is willing to lend a helping hand when you need help?

Her Majesty Keeps Her Word

Actions speak louder than words. Sometimes in networking events or when you meet or encounter someone, a person may promise one thing; however, they may not follow up or blow you away. This can happen. Not everyone can keep his or her word. But in life and business, your word is all that you have. So, make sure that when you say that you are going to do something for someone, make sure that you keep your word. If we do, however, make a mistake, it is important that we apologize for that mistake and make sure that we do not get caught in a sticky situation in the future.

Sometimes when people request things, it is better to say, "Let's see how that plays out; I'll get back to you," rather than a quick, "Sure yeah, that sounds like a plan" on the spot. By keeping your word, you build trust into all of your relationships. Just be extra selective in what you want to do for others. If you're not feeling like doing it, just don't do it.

Keep your life simple. No need to give an excuse as to why, just say, "I'm unable to do it," and move on. If you are able to do it, make sure that you notate it in your calendar, and make sure that the notion is realistic for you.

A Good Queen Knows a Thing or Two About Philanthropy

Volunteering in the community is a great way to get connected in your queendom. The best thing about it is that, you forget about yourself and now are focused on helping others. This is a great characteristic to have because it allows you to see life as a bigger picture. At times, we can feel like life is all about us, but really and truly it is about you and about others – they are not mutually exclusive. Make sure that whatever you choose to volunteer for, it is something that is worthwhile and that you have compassion for. Volunteer at a time when your heart is in it. If you have a given specialty or skill that can help others, by all means go and do it. Seeing someone smile and making that person's day just because you took that extra time to help them makes all the difference.

Based on my close relationship with God, I sometimes came across points in the scriptures that spoke about "who is greatest in the kingdom." I never understood the response when Jesus mentioned that the "greatest will be the least in the Kingdom of Heaven." Over time, I've come to understand that the greatest in the kingdom is the very least in the kingdom, and that is why those people that serve others the most are seen and recognized to be the greatest. Take a look at the great philanthropists of our times: Oprah, Mother Teresa, Bill and Melinda Gates, Warren Buffet, and countless others. They have spent time and money to help those in need, and have not taken their financial blessings for granted.

The Millennial Woman Utilizes Social Networks

In this great age of the transformation of communication into social media, the millennial woman is quite sensitive to her network. She knows that she is not the only one on this planet and reaches out to those that are in need. Not only does she 'like' a thing or two from her friends' photos. She will motivate and lead others into living a better life. One or two words of hope can change someone's life forever. She understands now that her social life has been extended to the Internet digitally and there are solutions and ways to speak to influence an anonymous audience. By knowing these things, she is able to be up to speed on technology and communication to influence her environment.

Now she is able to use her network, to push for greater opportunities.

Once you have attained your purpose, your social momentum will catapult you to your next opportunity. Building a social network takes time. With the newest social media platforms it can be overwhelming. I realized that the most important thing with these platforms are engagement. It doesn't mean how many people are only engaged with you, but really *how* engaged you are on these platforms. To be engaged online can be a full time job in itself, however if you love what you do, whether that is posting your latest outfit, or building your list of followers, keep in mind that building a network takes time and frequency.

I once studied this entrepreneur who created a water bottle product and *sold millions worth of her product all on Instagram!* What she did was create an account of fruit in water bottles and posted 3 times per day for one year. She never sold anything to her followers. After one year later, literally, she mentioned that she has a new water bottle product, and her fans went crazy! They were so excited that she was launching her glass water bottles they immediately pre-ordered. Within a time frame of 1.5 years of posting 3 times per day building her Instagram account, she sold millions worth of her product. I literally tracked every post she did (yes, I was that curious!) and looked at her engagement rate. I saw that she was engaging and sometimes tagged other instagram accounts that had similar pictures as she did. And that's that.

You have to start somewhere, even if it takes 24 months or 5 years or 10 years to accomplish your dreams. Always keep learning, and keep building.

CHAPTER 4

Demand Thy Throne

A Queen Diversifies Her Portfolio

There is now an increasing number of women working from home and being their own boss. One of the most proven ways of taking control of your life in general is to diversify your 9-5 and become an entrepreneur, if you are not one already. An entrepreneur is one who has started their own business and has taken control of their own financial freedom. One thing to know about working for someone forever is that the chances of having 100% autonomy in the life that you want to live is not as high as for the person that took the chance of becoming their own boss through investing in real estate or starting their own business. Although most queens are birthed into their high position of power, they still must be a steward of their money and grow the queendom. Even though some people have been born into financial stability, it is important to know that their ancestors were first entrepreneurs. It's always good to diversify.

Mass Job Stability Lasted Only a Century

Yes… the assembly line of the late 19th Century has spun out the mass production of cars, products, and jobs. However, although the previous generations have already went through labor union rights to live a nice stable job for the rest of their lives, we, however, have experienced the benefits of a mass-produced life and are seeing that job stability depends solely on the productivity of the company. As money is cut from a company's financial statements, they will either fire you, cut your hours, or make you work double to keep your job.

Although we Millennials have been born and taught that we must first have a great education to secure that most prominent career position to live a better life, it is best to know that NOW is the time to become an entrepreneur. We now comfortably have the world at our fingertips through the internet. Thousands of people are using the Internet or finding other ways of making money and working from home to live a more stable life.

The Golden Point: Part Time or Full Time?

By no means am I suggesting completely quitting your day job… yet. Lol. It all depends on your current position and how determined you are to accomplish your goals. There are numerous ways of making a living on the side, i.e. starting an online business, a traditional brick-and-mortar business, or a home-based business. However, it is important that, if you want to completely take control over your life, being a business owner is the way to go.

A great benefit of being a business owner is that you will start paying yourself in profits rather than hourly income. Once the business owner has a system that they worked hard to establish, after a certain time, they are then able to reap the harvest.

For example, if an owner of a wedding salon makes over $250,000/month in revenues, the owner will want her 12 bridal stylists to sell about $20,000 in wedding gowns *each*. When they hit quota, the owner pays her stylist 1% of $20,000 (which is… yes… $200) and keeps the other $19,800. She pays her rent and overhead (lets say 50%) and keeps the rest. So, she made about $10,000/stylist in cash profits. No wonder the stylists hardly see the owner!

This is a perfect example of the owner working smart rather than hard. Yes, she had to build the business from the ground up. However, after a certain time, she is able to administer her abilities and employ others to do what she can or cannot do. Imagine living a life of $10,000+/month, by providing a service that is beneficial and unique to others!

To go part-time or full-time into a business, time management is essential. We all have 24 hours in a day, and sleep for at least 8 of those. If we are able to use our talents and abilities to leverage our time, then we are able to further extend our time limit. In other words, if you utilize the tools that are provided online or adopt a system where you can leverage others' time, and not only rely on yours, then you have hit a golden point. You can be able to work wherever you want and live a life that you see fit.

You must also understand and adopt the risk vs. reward concept. Sometimes, high risk can reap high reward; however, remember that risk is also a PERCEPTION. What may seem risky to others may not seem risky to you, and vice versa. It's important to take an educated risk, and know what you are willing to give up to get to where you want to be. Is it time or money? If it is time or money, then what must you do to lower the risk?

Now, Your Majesty, Let's Saddle Your Horse, and Visit Your Bestie's (Habit) Infamous Learning Curve Castle

Ah yes, once you arrive at Habit's place, your bestie will show you her infamous learning curve roller coaster, which everyone goes on. It is always exciting. However, you might be a bit afraid of the "drop" once you go all the way to the top of the coaster, which I completely understand. This is what I'd like to call, the learning curve.

A learning curve is best described as discovering what you don't know and getting hit with the benefits and consequences of not knowing. (Btw, every consequence does turn into a benefit somehow eventually.) Sometimes, the best way to shorten the learning curve is to piggyback on someone else's experience so that you learn from them rather than learning all by yourself. This is the reason why I was so excited to work with a fashion industry expert and go to a top-notch fashion school, prior to thinking of launching my own high-end fashion line, Liselle Kiss. It is important to learn the business through mentorship, rather than jumping in to a new field and losing money.

Not every industry is the same, but the learning curve is very similar. Even if you know how to do something very well, turning that into a business or cash machine can be a learning curve in itself. So, I would highly recommend becoming an apprentice, reading books regarding your industry, and taking the time to write out a plan. I would highly recommend a business plan; however, don't get too overwhelmed with these details where it hinders you. Let the plan guide you, and revisit it later once you get a hold of things.

Give yourself time to learn and invest your time in these things. It may take a few weeks or months to get the hang of starting a new business but you will be an expert in your field which will be all worth the time.

Be Handed Your Golden Scroll of Purpose

Remind yourself everyday the reason why you get out of bed every morning. After giving yourself that fabulous wink in the mirror to have a wonderful day, be sure that you take time to revisit your purpose and why you do your labor of love. The "Why" is much more important in life than the "How." The "Why" can become a form of habit, and we can just lead ourselves into doing the things that we want to do, rather than thinking about "How" we did it.

Your bestie, Habit, really takes care of all of your "Why" moments. Think. What makes you tick, and makes you excited and happy for the day? Imagine the life that you feel that you deserve to live.... How does that make you feel? Can you see it? Taste it? Smell it? See it? How vivid is this vision of yours? Is it a movie or a picture? Imagine right now that you were able to accomplish this vision of yours....

This feeling of seeing and believing is a matter of the "Why." Your brain is smarter than you think. It knows how to complete a task without you understanding exactly how you did it. Once the "Why" is established, then the "How" will come. You will automatically see yourself doing the things that you must do to accomplish your purpose. Although the "How" is important to some extent, it is truly your brain's ability to focus and target that purpose to complete the function requested through Habit.

Your Majesty's suggestion: Action is needed, however, your vision is the catalyst for action.

To stick with your purpose and vision, you must write down your goals.

Your Majesty's Exercise, which she is mandated to perform at this very minute ;-)

Write out (with pen and paper) your dream life in 5 sentences. (Be sure to include work life, social life, love life, financial life, or other ambitions.)

Next, go ahead and write down how it would make you feel when you achieved all of these things.

Finally, take this sheet of paper and read it before you fall asleep. (A great way to summon Habit.)

Duty Calls: Focus on Your Strategy

One thing that is important is to keep focus on one thing at a time, to get quicker results. Although it sounds nice to be a renaissance woman and work on all things with all effort all at the same time, the reality is that when you focus on one thing at a time, you are much more efficient. So pick one of your purposes, and focus wholeheartedly on it until you've achieved it. Think of an Olympic athlete. They sacrifice countless hours to prepare for a competition, only for the hope of accomplishing their vision. Of course, they have to sacrifice their social life or finances to reach the epitome of their success. It all takes time, yet with persistence, you can reach it. When it comes to changing your mindset, you must focus on changing and adapting to the environment that you want to be a part of.

Let's Start out With Baby Steps....

One of the main reasons why I failed in the past was because I failed to realize the importance of baby steps. I fell into get-rich-quick schemes or other businesses where I thought that I would get a quick return on my investment within 6 months. I really and truly thought that I could just make it big, and that's it, no need to take little steps at all. Over time, I have seen businesses that actually grew so quick that it caused them to collapse just as quick. It was here, and now it's gone. Luckily, I have had the pleasure of being mentored by a smart businesswoman in the fashion industry, and I've realized the importance of taking baby steps.

My mentor told me that it is important to grow a company at a steady pace, as she already had many employees, a factory, and stores that wanted her clothing. She would warn me that it is important to grow steady, rather than too quickly, because if demand exceeded cash flow, the company would be at risk to tarnish its name as a provider and later would lose money in the process. I've seen her steadily grow her fashion business consulting division into a very stable company.

One thing at a time is what matters. Let Time be a friend, not an enemy. Think of *when,* rather than *if.* So, go ahead and list the steps that you *think* you must take to put yourself into action. You do not need to know EVERYTHING before you begin your own social media influence, home-based business, or freelancing career. Just go ahead and do it. Pick up the sticks along the way, and you'll run into the right people to direct you. It is just a given. Once you put it out there to complete your life purpose, everything will fall into place for you to achieve it. Just keep your vision, and take your time one step at a time.

Your Majesty's Pointers:

- Revisit your purpose, and make it solid
  - *Write your purpose in one sentence*
  - *Write down your top 5 goals within the purpose (write out your dream life in 5 sentences)*
  - *Write out long-term goals (5 years, 10 years…)*
  - *Visualize your end result*
  - *Be ok with baby steps*

Her Majesty chooses the way that she wants to do business

Fortunately, you are currently living and reading this book in the new millennium of the 2000's! Now you have the tools and resources that can propel you to monetize your influence, start-up or freelancing career into the most Time Efficient and Beneficial Business ever seen in history. With the advent of the Internet, now you can easily reach an audience whom you would never have thought of reaching. You, my lovely one, are living in a time of GREAT OPPORTUNITY, now freely given to the masses, once you decide to choose to live such a life. So, as the queen that you are, pick up your dazzling royal scepter and command what you want in life. Dictate the businesses that you want to be apart of or start. It's now your right to live out your birthright.

I would suggest to first start out by choosing the business model or career that you see fit. There are many ways that you can do business, and if you are currently doing business in any of these ways, mixing up the models is definitely an option.

Types of Online Businesses:

From my research of online business models, there are some in particular that you may look into replicating or being apart of.

Affiliate Marketing

The process of generating traffic for other websites and gaining a commission from the product or service bought from the traffic that you generated. This is an intricate process that takes being an expert in keyword search optimization, websites, and landing pages. This is a great way to generate passive residual income.

Research "best paying affiliate marketing programs" as a start to your research in affiliate marketing.

Freelance Service Provider

A service that is rendered that provides a product that is not physically tangible. This is also a great means of providing a freelancing service. This is like creating an app, website, a game, or providing a freelance internet based service for someone. Sometimes you can even gather the clients to assist and outsource some tasks to other freelancers to lighten the workload. They do this frequently in the digital marketing and advertising space.

Product Creator

Of course, for those fashionistas or crafty ones that want to provide a product to ship to their customers, then being a product provider is for you. One thing that I would like to stress to be weary of, is that it is important to not get too caught up with doing the shipping... y o u r s e l f. Trust me. With my t-shirt/tote bag business, I was the one that did all the shipping myself, and it was no fun. It is actually quite time consuming. The best suggestion is to OUTSOURCE the shipping via drop shipping, or hiring an ecommerce shipping company to do it. If you want to grow and have free time, it is critical to think of these things BEFORE you start your business. You can set things up where you ship it yourself for a couple of pieces, but please, after a certain bulk amount, set up drop shipping or outsource this process. Google "best drop shipping companies" and compare what works for you.

Please Note: This is not the dropshipping which is taking affiliate products from China on alibaba.com and marketing the same product online without purchasing it. That is another way to make money off of products that you *don't own*. This is more of the old school method of drop-shipping where you would find a company that will create the *original* item for you and DIRECTLY ship it to the customer (packaged the way you want – professionally and without the outsourced shipping company's name on it). Now that just sounds like a better piece of cake. I would like to have a slice of that please! :) Online t-shirt companies, promotional companies are a way that you can do this easily.

Information Provider

In the Information Age, people want information. Provide good information to people, and people will buy it. It is as simple as that. Thank goodness for the Internet. Now we are able to just go online and Google whatever we want, and we get it (most of the time.) So if you have a talent that people want to know "How-to" do, create a new website and generate interest in that topic. Create an e-book, e-course, or e-subscription service with your information. This builds passive income for you as well.

Diversify your online business portfolio

Please diversify your talent and time as well. If you are online and building a business, it is important to always keep an eye out for new opportunities. This can even mean switching from being only an information provider to adding products or services. Heck, go ahead and get affiliate marketers to work with you to generate traffic to your site. You can build an audience of affiliate marketers by finding influencers in your niche and ask them if they are interested in your promoting your product for a commission of 10%-50%. This depends on your margins, but if you are able to get 25 influencers to promote you with their special coupon code, it would be better than doing this all yourself. Creating a business is all about expansion, and if you're able to do that in a passive residual way, that is even better. It takes time to build something amazing, but when you do, it will be amazing. :)

Your Majesty Knows How to Keep a Royal Secret (shhhh!)

Also, in your business initiatives and ventures, please keep in mind that if you do come across an idea that is just out of this world, please be sure to keep this to yourself, until you protect yourself in the most proper way. :D

Be sure to trademark your brand, system or method, or even get a provisional patent to secure your idea. If you have an e-book, be sure to copyright it from the copycats out there. Copyright your website, i.e. at the bottom with year and company name. You are online and highly exposed.

Speaking of exposure, just because you are online, it is important to not feel like you're *that* incognito where you do not necessarily need to set up a legal business entity to protect your brand. A limited liability company is a great way to start your business, rather than only being a sole proprietor (claiming the business as yourself) so that you protect your personal assets properly. Starting a company has its own merits for tax purposes and protecting your personal assets.

Also, make sure that, when you are working to partner with a company or an individual to take your business to the next phase, be sure to have them sign a nondisclosure agreement or a non-compete agreement. Most people will sign a nondisclosure agreement, and if they refuse to, then that is definitely a red flag to look at. Non-compete agreements are great to use when you hire independent contractors or employees. The non-compete agreement discusses the penalties for using your ideas disclosed through the meeting or service rendered that the other party could use to their advantage and then directly compete against you. I've seen one of my good friends use this to his advantage, and he has protected his national territory from shark predators entering his niche financial loan market through his unique business concept.

Her Royal Majesty's Tools of Leverage That Your Majesty Didn't Quite Know… Yet… Lol

Power of Leverage

One thing that I am an advocate for is using the power of leverage to work more productively. The best way to leverage these days is to either hire someone next door or outsource your business needs to other people across the world or in your country, who will be more than happy to take the business. I suggest going to www.upwork.com or www.fiverr.com, to find professional people with great reviews at an affordable price to do what you would not or could not do.

I've used these wonderful resources constantly, and it just takes the pain away. :0

I mean seriously, if you need to get sales made, I recommend outsourcing your sales. Companies like www.timetohire.com is a great way to start. I once needed a sales superstar that was much better than me in sales. Yes, this individual had to be better, so that I could gain more productivity. I used Time To Hire and hired a gentleman that was twice my age with twice the experience who pulled in more than twice the amount of quality leads and sales than I could have done all by little self. Work smart, not hard is the philosophy.

Also as a start-up, when you do hire individuals, it is usually best to work with them starting off as an independent contractor. This allows them to do their own taxes, and all you do is pay them. Also, providing benefits is not something that you need to think much about either. Remember that the difference between an independent contractor and an employee is that the independent contractor *must* not be treated as an employee. They can take a vacation whenever they want and work with you when they want. They only must complete the terms or services agreed in the contract. If you want to start controlling your contractors with the hours they work, hire them as an employee. It's up to the company structure that you decided to put in place.

Power of automation

I am a student of automation through the studying of recent business automated systems. Have you ever wondered why when you sign up for an online subscription or an account, you start to receive emails regarding your topic of interest? Either these letters are meant to upsell you or just to keep you informed. There are automated systems that can be used to manage your future clients, such as Mail Chimp, and payment cycles like PayPal to receive automated payment. You can set up an email campaign of 8–10 emails when you have a new subscriber, or send them emails to inform them of your new blog posts. It is important to understand and use these resources to your advantage.

Imagine creating an e-course system to teach your niche, hobby, or interest to people who are genuinely interested in your product. I've seen these systems online priced at the "$x97" price, i.e. $97, $197, $597, $997, $1997 prices. Some are even based on monthly subscription pricing. I honestly believe that the price that you set does not matter. Price what you feel you deserve and build a clientele that will believe in your services. Price is relative.

Take a look at www.Udemy.com for examples of people that have created their own e-courses. Udemy is a great resource to create a platform for your e-course. However, I advise that you create your own website to protect your intellectual property as well. The more control you have over your platform the better it is for you in the long run. Be wary of the commission that you give out to your affiliates, publishers, or other third-party business partners.

Think automation. Once you have a life that is automated, with much less work in your life, wouldn't that mean more opportunities to focus on the things in your life that mean much more? This is true power, and there are thousands of people that are already doing this every day. Become a student of the automated business processes that work, and adopt these systems creatively into your business. Even though you've set up an automated business, you must always take a look at your baby and improve your automated system on a constant basis.

The Millennial Woman's Motto: Competition = Smallpetition

That's right! Competition = Smallpetition. Forget the little masses of competition – they have nothing to do with you. Opportunity is everywhere. Understand that life is not a competition. The competition is really with yourself. According to "The World's Billionaires," in 2014, there was a record 174 women billionaires, on a list of 1645 people. I'm not saying that you must hit billionaire status to feel as if there is no competition. I'm saying that every year, whether you're a billionaire or not, the economy is better than 100 years ago. Lol. Seriously. It only gets better from here. So go ahead, saddle your high horse, and take on the world! :)

CHAPTER 5

Thou Shalt Be Fed Grapes

Enjoy the Fruits of Your Labor

Recently, after hustling the New York life for about a year
(sometimes working 7–25 days straight), I decided to
pursue my life-long dream and travel to Europe. The timing
was perfect. *I bought my ticket the day before my flight to
Madrid.* Did I think 2 weeks or months before that I was
actually going to hop on a plane to Madrid within 24 hours
of deciding to go? Not quite. However, I did know that I did
deserve that trip, no matter what. I took a 3-week vacation
and told both of my jobs (as I had 2 part-time jobs) that I was
taking a vacation, no matter what. Thankfully, as the star
employee, it wasn't difficult to request time off. For those
who need more planning and time to let your boss know that
you gotta take that trip, make sure that you do to really enjoy
your vacation!

Sometimes, spoiling yourself is the best medicine. While you're laboring, it's important to take time for yourself to enjoy your fruit. We tend to use our efforts and time on the things that matter, but not quite on ourselves. We can overwork ourselves, be hard on ourselves, and rewarding ourselves with simple things, such as good food or a great movie, is nice. However, why not spend time with yourself as if someone else paid for it?

This what I think of as an inspirational fashion designer at Liselle Kiss. For a memorable shopping experience, I give an airline gift card to those who decide to collect my designer handbag. Why not combine shopping and travel? I feel that the wearer should not only experience a beautiful handbag, but she should also be able to enjoy her life because of it.

When there is peace and prosperity in the land, this is the time to continue to build up the foundation.

A solid foundation is continuously built so that when the time comes to defend yourself, you have layers of support within yourself. The best way to build this foundation within you is to stay grounded and make sure that wherever the wind blows, you will still be the queen and rule over your court. So, stay in control.

Here's what staying in control means:

- Being the ruler of your mind,
- Continuing to create your vision,
- Taking action according best intuition to get your desired end result.

Knowing that you have the ability to concentrate and be the ruler of your own thoughts and actions can take you further. Know what thoughts you are thinking when you are idle. Be aware of your positive thoughts and negative thoughts. When you receive a negative thought, question it. Why is it there, and what is the counter thought? Stay in control of your life, one thought at a time. Choose the thoughts and visuals, and feelings that you want to linger on for more than 1.5 minutes. If the thought isn't what you want, get rid of it immediately by concentrating on a new, more positive thoughts. Thoughts become strongholds when lingered on too long. Choose your stronghold, and diminish the old strongholds that you do not want by creating new counter strongholds through Habit.

When there are people around you whom you do not want to become or who bring you down, remove yourself from that environment, until you are able to control and re-make your strongholds to either influence the previous environment or to create a new one. This is the time to take care of you, to be around those people that will support your endeavors, and live out a life of fulfillment. We cannot live and breathe by ourselves to accomplish our goals and dreams, however. We need people that will support us, motivate us, and laugh with us.

While you are ruling your mind, you must continue to create your vision. Keep a foothold on what you want. Remember the feelings that you'll get once you accomplish this dream or goal. Know without a doubt that you have completed this task or dream, and be excited for the opportunities that are yet to come. Talk about your dreams to those who are close to you, and for the really juicy dreams, keep them to yourself. No need to give it all away. Create your vision boards, write in your journal, and stimulate yourself with great books and inspiration. Keep your eyes on the prize, the future you.

Who is the future you? What does she look like? How is she dressed? Who are her friends? What does she do? Where does she live? Where does she work? What does she eat? This is very important to define. Once you define who she is, act like her, talk like her, walk like her, be her, and eventually you will have made yourself into the future you. I had no idea 5 years ago that I would be jet setting to Europe, making friends all over the world, being an apprentice to a seasoned fashion designer, and paying off my debt for financial freedom. I finally have a brand new start, and it's because I took the time to analyze what were the pains of my life and what made me feel too comfortable to change these things.

I then realized that I must take action to create my new environment. Theory and thinking don't work by themselves. I must do the things that are uncomfortable to do. I had to tell my bosses while I worked in Miami that I wanted to demote myself to a part-time job so that I could find myself. I took less pay so that I could have the ability and freedom to create my future. No matter what, it all works out in the end. Yes, I made about $1000/month with over $1500 in expenses. However, the money came in at the right time every month. I definitely have God to thank for that, as I realized that there are some things that are beyond my control. When in need, trust in God, your Creator, who loves you so that everything else will follow.

Stay optimistic and hopeful. Know that when there is no way out, or if you're blocked, sometimes, it's a way to look up, see the light again, and later let the walls crumble.

However you decide to tap into your environment and take hold of the reigns of your world, go and take action.

Her Majesty's Favorite Pastime Is Being Spoiled

Yes, instead of waiting for someone to feed you your grapes, why not pick them yourself? No more need to wait for your birthday, anniversary, or holiday, to treat yourself. Take some time for yourself.

Once during a horrible break up, waiting by the phone, fantasizing, and hoping that that particular someone would see my value, I decided to take the boyfriend benefits and give them to myself. :-D So, because I was used to a good back massage, I went into Brookstone, bought a mechanical massager for my back, and took myself out to dinner with some friends, or by myself, depending on how I felt. Later, I realized that I'd never gone to a spa. So, I immediately booked the best spa package my neighborhood could accommodate. My spa day was one of the most memorable experiences, as I was invited by a welcoming staff, served complimentary champagne, given an electro-facial and full-body exfoliation with a vichy shower, and, to top it all off, given a spritz of dry jasmine oil.

My, did I feel like a princess (Jasmine)! ;-)

That was the moment that changed my perspective of how I ought to treat myself. It is best to treat yourself kindly and with the utmost respect. That way, if there is someone or a situation that tries to make you feel worse about yourself, remember how YOU treat yourself. A queen is treated as she feels she should be treated. Never settle, and expect nothing less than your best treatment.

So, go ahead and splurge $$$ for yourself. Take that random trip overseas, pat yourself on the back, and let no one ask you why you do these things. No need for an explanation, just let them know that you can do it, and that's that.

Also, remember to enjoy your loved ones, no matter how busy you are. Taking out the time to set a day with your friends and family is important. It's easy to get caught up with the fast life, especially while you're advancing towards your dreams. However, never forget those that have been with you before and those that are with you along the way. Not everyone around you can have the gusto that you put forth in life. You must always slow down, look back, and be with those who love you. Everyone has their own race at their own pace. So, no need to judge others if they're not up to par with your standards. Love those around you no matter what or where life takes them. Stay the course.

A Good Queen Knows That She Doesn't Know Everything

While you are eating your fruits, keep in mind that you must always handle and take care of your business. One mistake that I made post-college was not completely handling my business in the right manner or time. When I finally picked up my degree and moved from Orlando to Miami, I started to live the "adult" life. I was no longer a kid, and I had to fend for myself. At that moment, upon arriving in Miami, I was in search of a home. I knew that I could rent an apartment and just give away my $800/month to someone, or I could buy a house when the economy was down at its lowest in 2009.

Being 20 years old at the time, I was nudged by a friend to look into purchasing a property. I literally joked with him and told him, "Fine. I'm going to prank call the bank, and tell them I want to buy a home, with no work experience, fresh from college."

So, I called the bank, and they told me that I was pre-qualified for an FHA (Federal Housing Administration) loan! Because I was working as a Management Trainee at a rental car company and my business degree was related to my job, the bank would forego the necessary 2 years of work history!

Immediately, I jumped for joy. My credit was fair; I only had 2 credit cards below 40% of use, and student loans that I didn't need to pay for yet. All I needed was 3% down, and I could purchase my first home, up to $100,000.

I went on www.trulia.com to search for my property. I even found a great local realtor that was flexible with my crazy work schedule (most times, we viewed properties after dark with flashlights). Then boom – I found my perfect condo! It was a perfect 2/2 with great amenities – pool, Jacuzzi, security, gym, and tennis court. Originally on the market for $75,000 as a foreclosure, I bid it for $85,000 and won the bid. Now it was closing time. We closed the property 3 days before Christmas, and threw a painting-the-house party.

I kept my property for about 5 years and paid my mortgage until I had to move to New York. I placed tenants in, and later had problems with them paying. This delayed my cash flow while living in New York, and now I had to pay my mortgage in Miami, and my rent in New York City. Stressed out, I booked my flight from JFK to MIA to evict my tenants and even found a processor (a person that can complete the paperwork to evict tenants for you when you're far away) in the mix. After my tenants were gone, and now I had to pay for repairs (fridge was spoiled and the AC needed fixing). Even so, my mortgage was behind, and I owed the association a whopping $650/month because I was behind on payment.

Your Majesty's Advice: I would advise you to avoid properties with high association fees, especially as a new investor, because these fees can be burdensome on top of mortgage, and they will initiate punitive fees if you do not pay your fees on time.

Fortunately, I was able to re-rent my property to a good tenant, and eventually, I later sold the property for $135,000 and gained a profit. Although I suffered a major loss with association fees and over $10,000 in punitive damages, I still was able to sell my house without foreclosing. I'm very thankful for my realtor and mentors that were with me through this process. However, I learned that if I decided to take full responsibility in the matter in the beginning and not run away from paying those hefty bills, I would've gained over $10,000 for my bank account. It's really not worth it to get behind in debt and not pay your creditors. It'll drain the life out of you, and eventually there will be punitive damages while your credit score drops. Being young, I really didn't see the value or the big hype about taking care of my finances. Life before was such a dream – a blurry one. I just did whatever I felt like, whenever I felt like it, without thinking about the consequences of slacking or lagging on an important area. However, there is hope. There always is.

Her Majesty Keeps Her Crown by Earning Her Pendant of Responsibility

Whenever you find yourself in a pit, financially or emotionally, the best way is to look inward to find out exactly what is the fake truth that is keeping you in that fear of taking responsibility. Sure, there are external factors that will and can hinder you, but your reaction is your responsibility.

Responsibility = Fighting Action

Victimizing = Gutter Reaction

When a neighboring country attacks or if there is an internal revolution, you must brace yourself and be ready to take action. Sometimes life will back you into a corner, and you have no other choice but to find the strength to take up your royal sword and fight. The fight is usually predominantly internal. The best way is to strategize about your way of fighting, the way that you plan on taking action, so that you can win against your problems.

You will turn your problems into opportunities, your opportunities into solutions, and your solutions into breakthroughs.

Believe that you are in full control in that you take responsibility. This is what will separate you, and then you will free yourself to truly create your dreams. No one else cares about your dreams other than you. No one can tell you what is in your heart. Only you can feel the matters of your heart, so it is up to you to control your heart and focus on what truly matters to you. Life is more than just gaining. It is also important to have peace of heart and peace of mind.

The best way to take action is to listen to the people that have what you want. Do you have a friend or relative who is well off financially? Ask them how they manage their finances. Know someone that is living out the dream that you want? Ask them how they did it. The best thing when asking and seeking advice is to ask and listen to the people that are living out what you want. This means even to ask for and seek them out by association or by third-party inquiry. Do whatever it takes to know the correct answer in living out your life. NEVER take advice from someone who cannot relate to you, doesn't understand, or is simply not living out the life that you want. Their advice is just futile and a waste of your thoughts. Learn from the people that are living out their responsibilities.

One thing that one of my mentors mentioned to me, was that my sponge (brain) had become full. I already knew too much. However, the best way to release and squeeze out your sponge is to take action and do what it is that you learned.

Only action can allow you to put your dream into effect . Once your sponge is released, then you're able to grab more knowledge and know-how. Make sure that, no matter what, you keep on learning and keep on growing.

When Her Majesty Conquers the Territory, She Continues to Enjoy Her Journey

Finally, you've reached the Promised Land – your land of self-made promises, the land where dreams come true. The light of your dreams has finally reached the speckle in your eyes, and now you completely have it in the palms of your hands. You've been waiting all of your life for this one moment. You're here. You're finally here. It has been all these years. You've gone through so many struggles, so many ups and downs, heartaches, disappointments, and pain. Yet now, this is your moment, your glorious moment, the moment that only dreamers dream of, your dream that others laughed at or didn't believe. That dream has finally come true. Your dream is now your reality.

When you've arrived, know that you've arrived.

And now... it's time for you to dream again.

Yes love, when you accomplish your dream, that means that you've grown and now it's time to move on to the next big thing.

Your Majesty's Tip: Don't hoard your dreams and let them sit. Enjoy the fruits of your dreams for the moment, yet when it's time, get up and keep conquering.

Stronger. Better. Faster. Always achieve and always dream. After I came back from my vacation from Europe, I eased my way back into work. It actually felt like a 2-month long vacation, and I was ready to conquer other lands again after winning one of the greatest battles of my life – financial independence and peace of mind.

Your thoughts will now transition to:

- What else do I want?
- What are my other passions and dreams?
- What are some opportunities that I haven't taken advantage of yet?

My main philosophy in living out one's dreams comes from the "ask, seek, knock," principle from the passage below:

"So I say to you: Ask and it will be given to you; seek and you will find; knock and the door will be opened to you. For everyone who asks receives; the one who seeks finds; and to the one who knocks, the door will be opened."

–Luke 11:9-10

Think. Have you asked for what you want? Did you look for it? Are you taking action for it relentlessly? How large is your burning desire to achieve this dream of yours?

When You've Ruled Your Queendom, Pass on the Medallion to Others

Remember to never forget where you've been, and always remember where you were headed. Meanwhile, don't forget to pick up others along the way and help them get to their destination. Life is more than just *taking, taking, taking.* In reference to food, it's more like eating *tapas* style. We all share small plates so that we can try and learn the other flavors and so that we are all happy and satisfied.

When you start to live a life of abundance of opportunity, there will be many opportunities that will arise to help others. Finally, now you have the ability to help others when before you couldn't have helped yourself. You've reached the moment of fruition, where even your apples fall down to the floor so that others can benefit, and you don't mind. Not all of us have the same gifts and talents. However, we are able to share our gifts and talents as well. Whether this is knowledge, finance, or emotional support, this is a gift that we can give. One thing that is certain – what you give will come back tenfold.

The Millennial Woman Conquers Her Queendom

Your new woman within is now the ruler of your queendom. You are now fully aware of the thoughts and belief systems that have recently held you back. It takes time to create a new transformation, to form a new life, which feels surreal when you achieve it. Know this: When you start to live out your dream life, know that the dream will always continue; it will never fade, and it will always get better.

Take note of the baby steps that you've performed to get there, and stay on the big picture. The big picture will get you there much faster than focusing only on the small details. Since you've read this far, you've done well, as personal development is the key to reaching and growing onto a new horizon. Yes, we are blessed to live in this current generation, full of technological advancements and social opportunities like we've never seen before. But one thing that will never change is the possibility of who you will become. Take full advantage of every opportunity in front of you. Go, try out life, and sample it. Go travel places; pick up a new career or hobby just to expand your mind. Don't allow comfort to keep you in your place. As we grow older, we will be able to pass on our lives to future generations. This life is not only to live for us. We all cause butterfly effects. Every little thing that you set your eyes on will affect someone around you positively or negatively, indirectly or directly.

However, no matter how the environment may want to mold you into the situation, please always remember that it is always the power of your mind and your perspective that can change and alter your life. Your life will now change, if you so choose it. No matter which way the economy turns, every moment is an opportunity to take advantage of your new future. Don't let the worries of your life hold you back or take you down. Never settle; never give up, and if you ever feel overwhelmed, it is all right to retreat and reflect. A reflective life will help you tweak out the few areas of your life that could keep you from your dreams.

Be patient and know when to take action in all matters. Ask for what you want. One of the best ways to take action in what you want is to act the way that you want to act, dress the way that you want to dress, and visualize the life that you want to live. Know that whatever you want, you will get it, and don't let anyone tell you anything different.

Stay confident, cool, and collected, as the queen that you are, Your Majesty.

*Take note: I've provided an activity worksheet that will allow you to place into action what you've learned from this book. I want to make sure that you completely have all the tools and resources for you to accomplish your goals. I expect that Your Majesty will complete the assignments in the worksheet ASAP so that you can go and conquer!

Here's to your future conquered lands.

With Love,

Terri Liselle Kiss

The Liselle Kiss Dream-Catching Worksheet

Social Media Exercise:

Open up a LinkedIn account or start utilize your account more, and find people that you want to have in your circle. Start using yourFacebook account again to join a group that resonates with you or help you grow. For instance, if you want to learn how to be a better digital marketer, go to facebookad facebook groups. Send a quick hello, and take it from there. With Instagram, try to genuinely comment to 3 large influencers per day and view your engagement rate! Never use bots or software as that will hurt your account.

Volunteering Exercise:

What are you interested in helping to be a part of? List 3 things, and volunteer this WEEK!

Smiling Exercise:

Crack a BIG smile in the mirror for more than a minute. While smiling, act out in excitement for your new future reality. Then go take on the day!

Map out your Career Worksheet:

List 5 things that you love to do for fun.

List 1–3 things from your list that you could see yourself doing for a long time.

List out your skills (the skills that you do in your current job).

Which one of these skills do you enjoy doing? (Get creative! Mix a skill and your labor of love.).

How can you make money from this?

(Brainstorm and work to find business models similar to yours to imitate.)

How much money do you need, and do you really need to use it? (Think piggybacking – who can help you on their platform?)

Can you hire others to do it for you?

What resources are out there to ensure your success? (Think automation and marketing widgets.)

What are traits that you want your friends to have and that you look for within yourself (5 traits in your personality that attract great friendships).

The Settling Incubator:

Think of a few things in your life that you feel that you're settling with. Then write, in blue ink, the counter future action that make you feel that you're no longer settling.

Pinterest assignment:

Find and Pinterest your dream board. Share and follow others. Journal or write a paragraph of the feeling or motivation of the dream board.

Journal entry:

Write a journal entry in the future and get excited. Rate your excitement from a 1–10.

Mirror on the wall exercise:

List 3 new positive sayings about yourself to feel better about yourself.

Thankful exercise:

Write down 100 things that you're thankful for, no repeats. Reread your list twice.

Then gather your top 5 thankful reasons why you get out of bed. Write these down on an index card or sheet of paper.

Wandering Thoughts Test:

What are the top 5 things you think about when you're on your commute or relaxing in your favorite spot?

Write them down.

Also, try to catch those doubting thoughts and toss them away with a positive thought.

New Habits exercise:

What is a new habit you would like to start? Write it down in blue ink (retains information better).

Now, from there, write down 10 things that you are hopeful for.

How does it make you feel on a scale of 1–10?

Startup online business worksheet:

Pick your service (informative, product, service, affiliate marketing).

Research sites like the ones you would like to build.

Observe what works and what doesn't.

Pick what you like the most, and start your online business.

Stick to it; take your time, and analyze what works to spend as little money as possible in the beginning.

Responsibility Assignment:

What is the one thing in your life that you feel is holding you back? Have you taken responsibility for it yet? Write the one thing you can do to take action on this matter?

About The Author

erri Liselle Kiss is an inspirational fashion designer of Liselle Kiss. Terri Liselle has contributed for Entrepreneur.com, and has been a guest on various Sirius XM radio shows, and various media outlets. As a fashion designer she likes to focus on enhancing the lives of women while making them feel beautiful with her designer handbag line. Terri Liselle Kiss has an Associates of Fashion Design from Parsons at The New School, with a Bachelor's degree in Management specializing in entrepreneurship from the University of Central Florida. Liselle's startup experience and education has lead her into consulting individuals on product launches, as well as designing a high end collection for those who love cute handbags. She lives in New York City.

Credits

Cover photograph by: Djenabe Eduoard

Copyright

Made in the USA
Middletown, DE
27 October 2023